INSTANT TIN WHISTLE

About this book

THE TIN WHISTLE is a musical instrument possessing two special qualities: it is the *cheapest* and it's the *simplest*. However, don't be misled into thinking that it's barely more than a toy, or that it is inferior or a second-rate instrument.

On the contrary, despite its cheapness and its easiness for beginners, the tin whistle is a full-blooded musical instrument, capable of music of a quality often unsurpassed by far more eminent instruments.

In spite of this, the majority of people who acquire a tin whistle have only modest aims in view…indeed, most just buy on a passing whim; others, perhaps, receive a whistle as a gift.

For whatever reason, everyone who obtains a tin whistle and experiences a surge of enthusiasm is a potential player. *Sadly, far too many of these potential players are unable to fulfil their initial expectations.* Their enthusiasm fades and dies and their will to play is lost forever.

Ask yourself these questions:
1 Are you a potential whistle player?
2 Do you want to succeed?

If your answers are yes, then you shouldn't delay. You should use this book while that first spark glows. It will **grab, nurture** and **enflame** your enthusiasm, leaving you well and truly hooked. It has been carefully designed to substantially increase your chances of success.

HOW??????

By the use of a carefully formulated six-point plan, this book sets out to:

PRODUCE INSTANT RESULTS - the special whistle tablature means you are able to play the tunes right from the word **go!**

SUSTAIN INTEREST - the titles in this book have been carefully chosen to make sure that most people are familiar with most of the tunes. Thus, your attention will be held throughout the initial vulnerable period of learning and you can build up a reasonably sized repertoire quickly.

INTRODUCE TRADITIONAL MUSIC - the kind of music 'the whistle does best'. A few hand-picked traditional tunes have been included, to get you started on the 'real journey'.

PROMOTE ENJOYMENT - the inclusion of words and guitar chords and the encouragement to play with others will give you the chance to realise just how much fun music really is.

STIMULATE LEARNING - illustrations are included in the book which will focus your attention on the information which they surround. This will increase your chances of learning at least some of the playing hints and the music theory that the book provides.

ENCOURAGE FURTHER RESEARCH - although instructions in the book have been kept to a minimum and as simple as possible, just a smattering of advanced information has been included, to inspire you to learn more.

GW00538378

THE SOUNDTRACK

This book can be used on its own. However, to make learning the tin whistle even easier, a recording of all the tunes, plus the grace notes, has been produced. Each tune is played slowly, twice through and features guitar accompaniment using the chords shown in this book.

By altering the balance control on your player, you can make either the tin whistle or the guitar louder and so join in!

Order the soundtrack (DMPCD9610) or obtain details of other publications by contacting the publisher direct:

mally.com 3 East View, Moorside Cleckheaton, West Yorkshire BD19 6LD, U.K.
Telephone: +44 (0)1274 876388
Fax: +44 (0)1274 865208
Email: mally@mally.com
Web: http://www.mally.com

DON'T DELAY - START TODAY!

Instant Tin Whistle

The note B

The note A

The note D

The note G

The five lines upon which music is written are known as the **stave.** The **pitch** of a note is indicated by its position on the stave.

The note B (shown to the left) is found on the **middle** line of the stave.

Practise playing this note. Place the mouthpiece of the whistle between your lips, not your teeth, cover the first hole with the first finger of your *left* hand and gently blow a steady stream of air. Experiment with different pressures until you produce a nice clear note.

Now play the note A (shown below left) by covering the first two holes and play the first few notes of *Jingle Bells.*

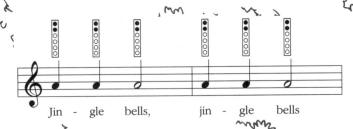

Jin - gle bells, jin - gle bells

Separate the notes by saying 'te' before each one ('te' as in 'le**tte**r'). This is known as **tongueing.** Notice that some notes naturally last longer than others.

The note for 'bells' lasts twice as long as the others. Time duration is indicated by using different note symbols.

The solid notes ♩ are called **crotchets.**

The hollow notes ♩ are called **minims.**

The duration of minims is **twice** that of crotchets. ♩ = ♩ + ♩

Now play the note shown to the left, the hardest note of all, the low D. Make sure all the holes are completely covered, then blow **gently.** Ensure that you are using the first three fingers of your left hand to cover the three holes nearest the mouthpiece and the first three fingers of your right hand to cover the remaining three holes; rest your two thumbs at the back, behind your first or second fingers.

Now play this little tune, tongueing each note.

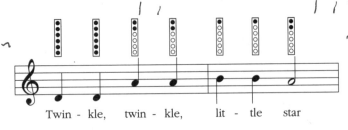

Twin - kle, twin - kle, lit - tle star

The symbol found at the beginning of each line of music is called a **treble clef.** Music for the whistle will always have this symbol at the beginning.

Music is divided into small sections by vertical lines across the stave. These sections are called **bars.**

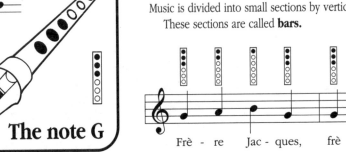

Frè - re Jac - ques, frè - re Jac - ques

2

The symbol ♯ is called a **sharp**; it raises the pitch of a note by one **semi-tone,** the smallest interval of musical pitch.

Sharps are the **black** notes of the piano.

F is automatically sharpened to F sharp on the D whistle.

Lon - don bridge is fal - ling down

The unfamiliar note in the music above ♪ is called a **quaver.**

Quavers have a duration **half** that of crotchets. ♩ = ♪ + ♪

A **dot** increases the duration of the note it follows by a half, for example ♩. = ♩ + ♪ or 𝅗𝅥 = ♩. + ♪

When quavers occur in groups, they are usually joined together by a **beam** as shown below in *Old King Cole.*

Old King Cole was a mer - ry old soul

The D note shown below right is said to be an **octave** higher than the D note learned previously.

To play this note and others in the high octave, you will need to blow somewhat harder to get the correct sound; this is indicated by an **asterisk** over the whistle symbol throughout the book.

Land - lord fill the flow - ing bowl

Because no holes are covered to produce the note C sharp, supporting the whistle can be difficult. However, notice that covering the last hole on the whistle, whilst playing the C sharp, doesn't affect the pitch. Thus, the hole can be covered to support the whistle when the C sharp notes occur.

Now play the scale of D major, the natural scale of the D whistle, from the bottom to the top and back again, using all the notes learned so far.

doh ray me fah soh lah te doh

F sharp (F♯)

The note E

High D

C sharp (C♯)

3

The notes of music are named in ascending order after the first seven letters of the alphabet. After G, we begin again with A.

Notes on the whistle can be played in two octaves. Don't forget, notes in the high octave, denoted by the asterisk, require more air pressure.

High E

High F sharp

High G

The note C

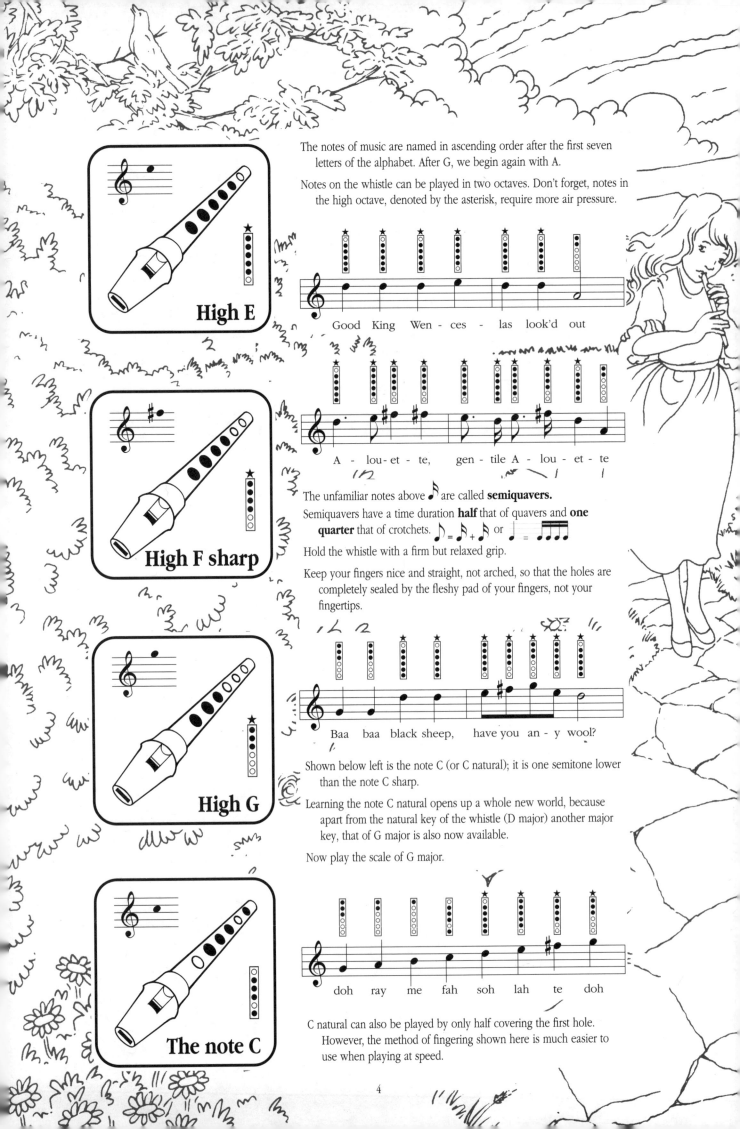

Good King Wen - ces - las look'd out

A - lou - et - te, gen - tile A - lou - et - te

The unfamiliar notes above ♪ are called **semiquavers.**

Semiquavers have a time duration **half** that of quavers and **one quarter** that of crotchets. ♪ = ♪ + ♪ or

Hold the whistle with a firm but relaxed grip.

Keep your fingers nice and straight, not arched, so that the holes are completely sealed by the fleshy pad of your fingers, not your fingertips.

Baa baa black sheep, have you an - y wool?

Shown below left is the note C (or C natural); it is one semitone lower than the note C sharp.

Learning the note C natural opens up a whole new world, because apart from the natural key of the whistle (D major) another major key, that of G major is also now available.

Now play the scale of G major.

doh ray me fah soh lah te doh

C natural can also be played by only half covering the first hole. However, the method of fingering shown here is much easier to use when playing at speed.

4

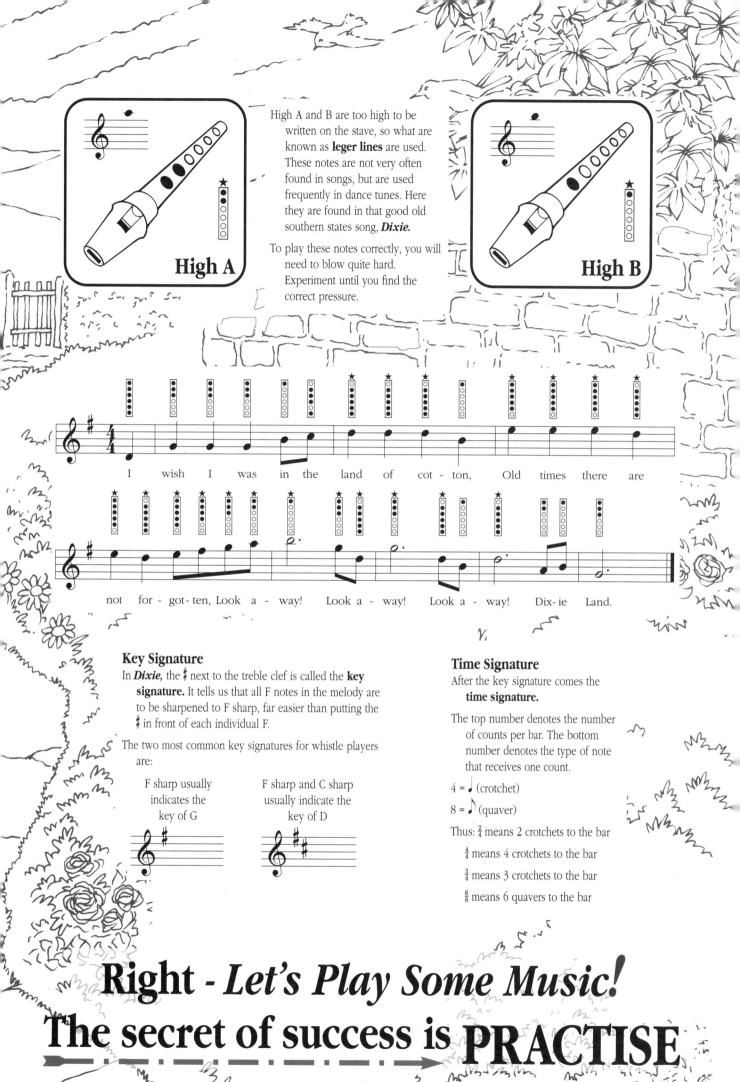

High A

High B

High A and B are too high to be written on the stave, so what are known as **leger lines** are used. These notes are not very often found in songs, but are used frequently in dance tunes. Here they are found in that good old southern states song, *Dixie.*

To play these notes correctly, you will need to blow quite hard. Experiment until you find the correct pressure.

I wish I was in the land of cot-ton, Old times there are not for-got-ten, Look a - way! Look a - way! Look a - way! Dix-ie Land.

Key Signature

In *Dixie,* the ♯ next to the treble clef is called the **key signature**. It tells us that all F notes in the melody are to be sharpened to F sharp, far easier than putting the ♯ in front of each individual F.

The two most common key signatures for whistle players are:

F sharp usually indicates the key of G

F sharp and C sharp usually indicate the key of D

Time Signature

After the key signature comes the **time signature**.

The top number denotes the number of counts per bar. The bottom number denotes the type of note that receives one count.

4 = ♩ (crotchet)

8 = ♪ (quaver)

Thus: $\frac{2}{4}$ means 2 crotchets to the bar

$\frac{4}{4}$ means 4 crotchets to the bar

$\frac{3}{4}$ means 3 crotchets to the bar

$\frac{6}{8}$ means 6 quavers to the bar

Right - *Let's Play Some Music!*
The secret of success is PRACTISE

Rudiments of music

Chromatic scale

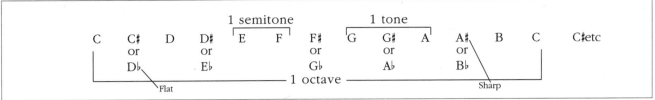

Treble clef

Music symbols

Counting time & note values

Counting time

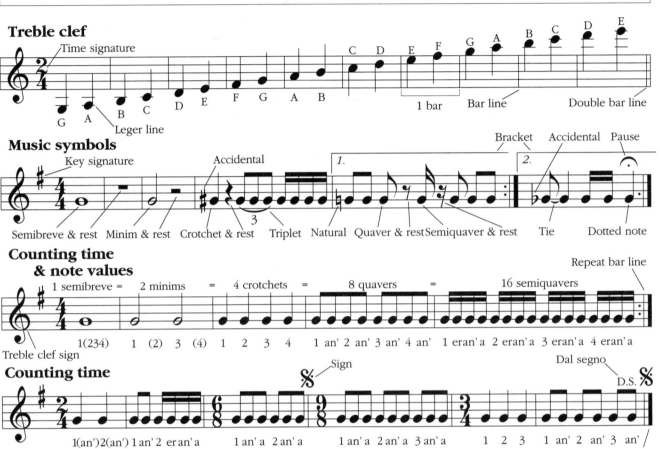

Glossary

Chromatic scale — consists entirely of semitones.

Diatonic scale — consists of a series of notes from the chromatic scale at set intervals, e.g. the major scale (do-re-me etc) has intervals of: *tone, tone, semitone, tone tone, tone, semitone*. Thus the scale of C is **C, D, E, F, G, A, B, C** and the scale of D is **D, E, F#, G, A, B C#, D**. Tunes take all or most of their notes from a particular diatonic scale. Each scale has its own set number of sharps or flats.

Key signature — shows which notes have to be sharpened or flattened. It also gives an indication of the key. Keys are named by the first note of the scale.

Accidental — is a note which is altered to *sharp, flat* or *natural* and is foreign to the key indicated by the key signature. An accidental sign applies to the note it precedes and, unless contradicted, all further notes of that pitch up to the end of the bar.

Time signature — resembles a fraction. The top number indicates the number of beats per bar; the bottom number indicates the time unit for the beat
(2 = a minim, 4 = a crotchet, 8 = a quaver, 16 = a semiquaver). For example, $\frac{4}{4}$ = 4 beats per bar occurring every crotchet.

Rest — denotes a period of silence, of specified length.

Triplet — consists of three notes played in the time of two of the same value.

Tie — joins two notes of the same pitch and denotes a single sustained note with a time value of the two combined.

Dotted note — a dot placed after a note lengthens that note by half. Thus

Double bar line — marks the end of an individual section or part of a tune. A 'final' bar line can indicate the end of a piece or the end of a principal section. A final bar line preceded by two dots indicates that that particular section has to be repeated.

Bracket — play the bar under '1' the first time through; substitute the bar under '2' on the repeat.

Dal segno — return to the sign and repeat.

Fine — (pronounced 'feenay') means end.

Chord formations

Chord	B♭	F	C	G	D	A	E	B	F#	Gm	Dm	Am	Em	Bm	F#m	C7	G7	D7	A7	E7	B7
Root	B♭	F	C	G	D	A	E	B	F#	G	D	A	E	B	F#	C	G	D	A	E	B
Third	D	A	E	B	F#	C#	G#	D#	A#	B♭	F	C	G	D	A	E	B	F#	C#	G#	D#
Fifth	F	C	G	D	A	E	B	F#	C#	D	A	E	B	F#	C#	G	D	A	E	B	F#
Seventh																B♭	F	C	G	D	A

Skip to my Lou

Tap your foot at an even pace, say one tap per second and count **1**, 2, 3, 4, **1**, 2, 3, 4 and so on. Each count is one crotchet; minims have two counts. Two quavers share a count; use the word 'and' (say an') to count quavers that don't fall on the main beats.

Play these early tunes using the tongueing technique to produce crisp, clear notes. Don't forget, you're looking at the symbols on the page as if in a mirror; the top of the symbol is the end nearest your lips.

A double bar line denotes the end of a section.

Counting 4/4 time

1 2 3 4 1 (2) 3 an' 4 an' 1 (2 3) 4 1 (2) an' 3 4

Chords used in this song:

D   A7

D   D   A7   A7
Lost my lov - er, what'll I do? Lost my lov - er, what'll I do?

D   D   A7   D
Lost my lov - er, what'll I do? Skip to my Lou, my dar - ling.

D   D   A7   A7
Go now, skip to my Lou, Go now, skip to my Lou,

D   D   A7   D
Go now, skip to my Lou, Skip to my Lou, my dar - ling.

7

Bobby Shaftoe

Count **1** an' **2** an' **1** an' **2** an' etc.
Use the syllable 'er' to count the semiquavers.

Ignore the curved lines on the stave for now, they simply show that a singer uses more than one note for a word.

Chords used in this song:

G   D7

G
Bob - by Shaf - toe's gone to sea,____ Sil - ver buck - les on his knee,____

He'll come back and mar - ry me,____ Bon - ny Bob - by Shaf - toe.

Bob - by Shaf - toe's bright and fair, Comb - ing back his yel - low hair,

He's my ain for ev - er mair, Bon - ny Bob - by Shaf - toe.

Donkey Riding

Guitar accompaniment

Usually melodies are not played or sung solo, they have accompaniment. Why not find a friend who plays guitar to accompany your tunes? You will find your music becomes much more fun and rewarding playing with others.

To facilitate this, guitar chord names have been included under the stave. The chord shapes these represent can be found on both the back cover as well as in a separate box on each page.

Chords used in this song:

G   Am   C   D

G — Were you ev - er in Que - bec, Stow - in' tim - ber on the deck,
Am — G — Am — D

G — Where you'd break your own dear neck, A - rid - ing on a don - key!
Am — G — Am — D — G

C — G — Way, hey a - way we go, Don - key rid - ing, don - key rid - ing,
Am — G — Am — D

C — G — Way, hey, a - way we go, Rid - ing on a don - key!
Am — G — Am — D — G

9

New York Girls

Chords used in this song:

G   C   D7

Lead-in bar

The sum of the notes in bars of music is always equal to the amount indicated by the time signature. Bars of $\frac{2}{4}$ time contain 'two crotchets-worth' of notes; bars of $\frac{3}{4}$ time contain 'three crotchets-worth' etc.

Most songs and tunes start just before the main beat occurs, so there is usually a short 'lead-in' bar at the beginning. This short bar becomes part of the last bar on repeating. The notes missing from the last bar are found in the 'lead-in' bar.

G · · · · · · · · · C · · · · · D7 · · · · · G · · · · ·

As   I   walk'd   down   the   Broad-way,   one   ev'n   ing   in   Ju   -   ly,   I

G · · · · · · · · · C · · · · · D7 · · · · · G · · · · ·

met   a   maid,   she   ask'd   me   trade,   a   sail - or   John   said   I_____   and   a-

G · · · · · · · · · C · · · · · D7 · · · · · G · · · · ·

way,   you   San - te,   my   dear   An - nie,

G · · · · · · · · · C · · · · · D7 · · · · · G · · · · ·

All   you   New   York   girls,   can't   you   dance   the   pol - ka?

Black Velvet Band

Counting ¾ time

Count **1**, 2, 3, **1**, 2, 3, etc. Use an' to count the quavers.

Tie

In this tune we find notes joined together by a **tie**. A tie joins notes of the same pitch, indicating a single sustained note, with a time value of the two (or more) combined. Turn the page for an explanation of the curved line joining notes of a *different* pitch.

Chords used in this song:

G   C   A7   D7   D   Em   Am

As I was walk - ing down Broad - way,_____ In -

G   G   C   G   G

tend - ing not long for to stay,_____ Well, then

G   A7   D7   D7

who'd I meet but this fair young maid, Come

G   D   Em   Em

trip - ping a - long the high - way?_____

Am   D   G   G

11

Sam Hall

Chords used in this song:

G C D G7 Am Em

In this tune we find a new kind of note: o It is called a **semibreve.** It has a time duration equal to that of four crotchets, i.e. a count of 1, 2, 3, 4.

Slurring

Now you are familiar with tongueing, try playing tunes using a steady stream of air. This technique is known as **slurring.**

A good place to practise the slur in this tune is indicated by the curved lines in the first and third staves of music. This type of curved line is, conveniently, called a **slur** and is distinct from a tie. Often, it is used as an indication to singers to draw a syllable out over the notes it encloses. Fiddle music has them to advise players not to change bow direction during those notes.

You'll encounter more slurs from later on in the book. To help you when reading at speed, if there isn't a whistle symbol over the note, then the curved line is a tie. If there **is** a symbol, the curved line is a slur.

The best whistle players slur nearly all of the time, using tongueing as a feature or to separate consecutive notes of the *same* pitch.

12

The Nightingale

Grace notes

Now try another method of separating notes of
the same pitch, by the use of **grace notes.** A
grace note is a quick note which steals its
time from the note it precedes. It is
produced by a quick flick of a finger. Try
separating notes of the same pitch in this
tune by quickly playing the note above or, if
you prefer, the note below. Playing the note
below is often called **tipping** or **striking.**

Don't forget, though, that
the notes joined by the
slur will sound best
when played in one
continuous breath.

Chords used in this song:

G   D7   D   C   Am

Oh, my sweet-heart, come a - long, don't you hear the found song, The sweet notes of the

G   G   G   G   G

night - in - gale flow? (Tra - la - la) Don't you hear the fond tale of the sweet night - in -

D7   G   D   G   C   G

gale, As she sings in the val - ley be - low?

D   G   Am   G   Am   G

As she sings in the val - ley be - low?

D   G   D7   G   G

13

Reuben Ranzo

More on grace notes

A far more common type of grace note is that known as the **cut.** It can be executed on all the notes except C natural and C sharp.

The notes D, E, F sharp and G are cut by A. Play the main note, then lift the third finger of the left hand for an instant, then quickly snap it down whilst still playing the main note. The notes A and B are cut by C sharp, by raising and quickly snapping down the first finger.

Listen to the soundtrack (see page 1) to get a better idea of how grace notes should sound.

These cuts are executed in exactly the same manner when playing in the higher octave. As well as being used to separate consecutive notes of the same pitch, cuts can be used anywhere in the tune at the player's discretion. They help make the melody more attractive and interesting.

The cut is the simplest form of the ornamentation which plays such a vital role in the performance of traditional dance music. Try to introduce cuts and other grace notes, where the fancy takes you, to embellish the tunes found in this book.

Chords used in this song:
G D Am D7

Ran - zo was no sail - or, (G / D / G) Ran - zo me boys, (Am) Ran - zo, (D) He

shipp'd on board a whal - er, (Am / D7 / G) Ran - zo me boys, (G / D) Ran - zo. (G)

The transposing instrument

The tin whistle is a transposing instrument. A basic few finger patterns are used which, once learned, can easily be transferred to whistles of other pitches. Given a half-a-dozen whistles of different sizes, this means you can play in **any** key using no more than the five easiest fingering patterns: very useful in a band situation. In other words, it's not necessary to learn how to play in all twelve keys on just one instrument, which you would have to do on a piano or fiddle. The easy keys on a D whistle are shown on the cursor above right. They're called the **nominal** keys. On the D, they're also the **actual** keys.

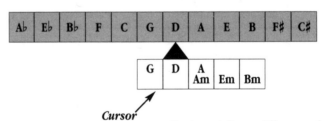

| Ab | Eb | Bb | F | C | G | D | A | E | B | F# | C# |

| G | D | A / Am | Em | Bm |

Cursor

Let's say you have a whistle in C. If you transfer the cursor to a piece of card and then line up the arrow with C, you will find that if you use your normal (i.e. nominal) fingering for G, the actual key produced is F.

Coming at it from a different angle, assume the singer says, "This song is in F." You could in fact choose one of three whistles, but let's also assume that the only other whistle you have is a Bb. Point the arrow to Bb and the cursor tells you to use your nominal **A** fingering for the tune to come out in the key of **F**.

South Australia

Breathing

Don't just stop anywhere to take a breath; try to make your breaths part of the tune. Draw breath at or near the end of a phrase by dropping or shortening a note. There are no hard and fast rules on breathing and phrasing, but 2 or 4 bar phrases are the most common. In some tunes you may like to use solely 2 bar phrases; in others you might use two 2 bar phrases, followed by one 4 bar phrase and so on.

Listen to good traditional players and experiment to find the best breathing points.

Chords used in this song:

G D C

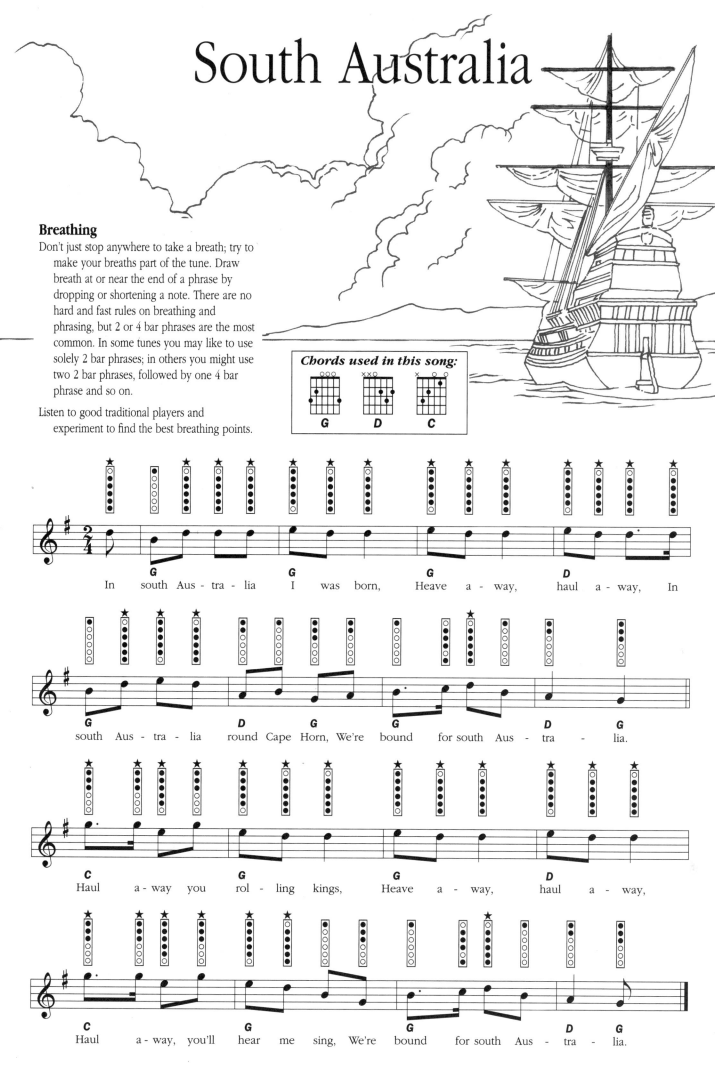

In south Aus - tra - lia I was born, Heave a - way, haul a - way, In

south Aus - tra - lia round Cape Horn, We're bound for south Aus - tra - lia.

Haul a - way you rol - ling kings, Heave a - way, haul a - way,

Haul a - way, you'll hear me sing, We're bound for south Aus - tra - lia.

The Leaving of Liverpool

Chords used in this song:

D   G   A7

The best whistle players are those who manage to strike the ideal balance of tongueing and slurring, introduce a tasteful amount of ornamentation – whilst vigilantly avoiding excess – and make breathing a feature, rather than a troublesome necessity.

Fare thee well to Prin - ce's land - ing stage, Riv - er Mer - sey, fare thee well,_____ I am

bound for Ca - li - for - ni - ay, It's a place that I know right well._____ So it's

fare thee well, to my own true love, When I re - turn, u - nit - ed we will be,_____ It's not the

leav - ing of Liv - er - pool that grieves_____ me, But my dar - ling when I think of thee._____

Fathom the Bowl

Fingering hints

Covering the last hole of the whistle has no effect on the notes A, B and C sharp. When playing these notes, it is often useful to keep this hole covered to give the whistle extra support.

It is not necessary to leave the first hole uncovered when playing the high D. Experiment as to when and where not to cover it.

Use your new-found knowledge to amend the fingering of this and of other tunes in the book.

Chords used in this song: D A E7 A7 G Em

Come all you loy-al her-oes give an ear to my song, And I'll sing in the
praise of good bran-dy and rum, There's a clear crys-tal foun—-tain in Eng-land shall
flow,—— Bring me the punch la-dle, I'll fa-thom the bowl. I'll fa-thom the
bowl, I'll fa-thom the bowl, Bring me the punch la-dle, I'll fa-thom the bowl.

All for me Grog

Counting $\frac{6}{8}$ time

Hump - ty Dump - ty sat on a wall

$\frac{6}{8}$ time is easiest understood by
using the rhythm of the words
to *Humpty Dumpty.*

Chords used in this song:
G C D

And it's all for me grog,————— me jol - ly, jol - ly grog,—————

All for me beer and to - bac - ca,————————— For I've

spent all me tin on the las - ses drink - ing gin, And a -

cross the west - ern o - cean I must wan————————— der.

The Old Woman from Wexford

Double-tongueing

When encountering a series of short, quick notes at tempo, particularly when they are the same pitch, it may be appropriate to use a little trick called **double-tongueing.**

Instead of tongueing each note with the syllable **te**, alternate **te** with the syllable **ke** as in jo**ke**r. Make use of this technique as indicated in the first bar of this tune.

Chords used in this song:

D   A7   G   A

Well, there was an old wo-man from Wex - ford, in Wex - ford town did

dwell,_____ She lov'd her hus - band dear - ly, lov'd a -

no - ther twice as well, With me right-fol lid - dle ee -

air - y, with me right - fol lol - de - ra.

Whiskey in the Jar

All the tunes so far have been in **major keys**. This tune is no exception - two sharps in the key signature and the last note being D indicate that this tune is in the key of D major.

Rests

A rest in music is a period of silence. The rest symbol denotes a period of silence equivalent to one crotchet.

Chords used in this song:

D   Bm   G   A   D7

As I was go-ing o - ver the far-famed Ker-ry moun-tains, I met with Cap-tain Far-rel and his

mon-ey he was count-ing, I first pro-duc'd my pis-tol and then pro-duc'd my rap-ier, Says,

"Stand and de - li-ver for you are a bold de - cei-ver," Mush-a ring-um-a doo-rum da, *(Clap, clap, clap,*

clap) Whack fol the dad-dy - o, Whack fol the dad-dy - o, There's whis-key in the jar.

Home, Boys, Home

One sharp in the key signature and the last note being G indicate that this tune is in the key of G major. G and D are the two main major keys available on the D whistle.

The rest symbol 𝄾 denotes a period of silence equivalent to one quaver.

Chords used in this song:

G   C   D   D7   G7   A7

G   G   C   G   D   D7   G   D

Now who would- n't be a sail - or lad, a- sail- ing on the main,___ To earn the good- will of our cap- tain and trade?_ Well,

G   C   G   D   D7   D7   D7   G

we went a- shore, on one eve- ning for to be,___ And that was the be- gin- ning of my own true love and me. And it's

G   D   G   D   G   G   G7   C   G   A7   D7

home,__ boys,__ home, *(Clap, clap)* Home I'd like to be,__ home for a while in my own coun- ter - y, Where the

G   C   G   D   D7   D7   D7   G

oak and the ash and the bon- ny i- vy tree,__ Are all grow- ing green- er in my own coun- ter - y.

Johnny, I hardly knew Yeh!

As well as major keys, there are also **minor keys.** This tune is in the key of A minor. Many traditional dance tunes are in minor keys.

Chords used in this song:
Am   Em   C   G   F   E7

Am   Am   Em   Em
While going the road to sweet Ath - y, a - roo,_____ a - roo,_____ While

Am   Am   Em   Em
going the road to sweet Ath - y, a - roo,_____ a - roo,_____ While

C   G   F   E7
going the road to sweet Ath - y, A stick in me hand and a tear in me eye, A

Am   G   F   E7   Am   Am
dole - ful dam - sel I did spy, John - ny, I hard - ly knew yeh!_____

Whip! Jamboree

This tune is written in the key of E minor. A and E are the main minor keys available on the D whistle.

Use double-tongueing to play the groups of four quavers.

Chords used in this song:

Em   G   D

Whip! Jam - bo - ree, whip! Jam - bo - ree, With your pig - tail, sail - or, hang-ing down be - hind, Whip!

Jam - bo - ree, whip! Jam - bo - ree, Oh, Jen - ny get your oat-cakes done.____ And

now Cape Clear it is in sight, We'll be off Hol - y-head by to - mor - row night, And we'll

shape our course for the old Rock light, Oh, Jen - ny get your oat-cakes done.____

Love is Teasing

The C sharps in this tune are foreign to the key indicated by the key signature. They are called **accidentals**. An accidental sign applies to the note it precedes and, unless contradicted, all further notes of that name up to the end of the bar.

Chords used in this song:

G · D · D7 · E7 · A7 · C

Oh, love_____ is teas - ing and love is please_____ - ing, And

love is a pleas - ure when first_____ it's new,_____ But

as love grows ol - der then love grows col_____ - der,_____ And

fades_____ a - way like the morn_____ ing dew._____

Maggie May

With the exception of the note C, notes learned so far occur in the **natural** key of the whistle. The remainder of the chromatic scale (see *Rudiments of Music* on page 6) can be played by only **half** covering particular holes. The A sharp encountered here is played by only half covering the second hole. This is achieved by pulling the finger away slightly, or by straightening the nearest joint to the fingertip.

Experiment with the finger position until you can play the note correctly. ***Note:*** don't try to half hole in the manner that could be construed from the whistle symbol; it has been represented in this way solely for clarity - see the back cover.

Chords used in this song:

D G E7 A7 D7

I was paid off at the home from a voy'ge to Sierr' Le - one, And two pounds ten and six-pence was me pay, As I

D   D   G   G   D   E7   A7 A7

jin-gled with me tin, Well, I was v'ry soon ta-ken in, By a girl by the name of Mag-gie May. Oh,

D   D   G   G   A7   A7   D   D7

dirt-y Mag-gie May, they have ta-ken you a - way, For to slave up-on Van Die-man's cru-el shore, For you've

G   G   D   D   D   E7   A7   A7

robb'd so ma-ny sail-ors and you've skinn'd so ma-ny whal-ers and you'll ne-ver walk down Lime Street a-ny more.

D   D   G   G   A7   A7   D   D

Camptown Races

Chords used in this song:

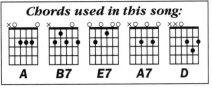

A B7 E7 A7 D

In addition to the major keys of D and G, the key of A major can also be played on the D whistle. This key has three sharps, F, C and G, so don't forget all Gs are now sharp.

This particular tune is easy because there are no G sharps to contend with. It was composed by Stephen Foster around 1849. He wrote many songs that are still popular, such as *Beautiful Dreamer* and *Oh! Susanna*.

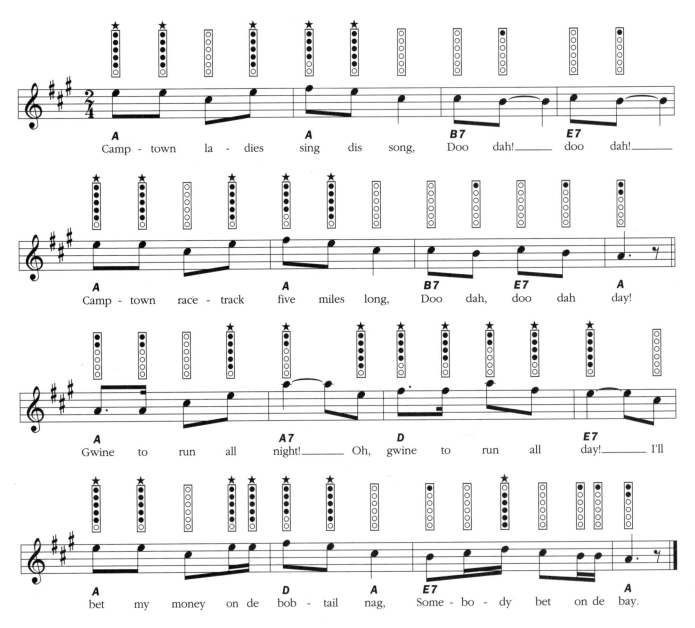

A — Camp-town la - dies sing dis song, Doo dah!____ doo dah!____

A — Camp-town race - track five miles long, Doo dah, doo dah day!

A — Gwine to run all night!____ Oh, gwine to run all day!____ I'll

A — bet my money on de bob - tail nag, Some-bo-dy bet on de bay.

Who's the Fu' Now?

Here is another tune in A major. Don't forget that G is sharp. G is sharpened by only half covering the third hole.

Chords used in this song:

A   E7   D   E

Mar - tin said to his man, "Fie, man, fie,"
A   A   A   A

Mar - tin said to his man, "Who's the fu' now?"
E7   E7   E7   E7

Mar - tin said to his man, "Fill thou the cup and hide the can,
A   D   A   E7

"Thou art well drunk - en, man, Who's the fu' now?"
A   D   E   A

27

Speed the Plough

So far, we have been playing easy, well-known song tunes. These have provided an enjoyable means to quickly become familiar with the tin whistle, but it is now time to move on. The tin whistle, despite its humble appearance, can be used to play very intricate and complex melodies; in the hands of a master, it is capable of rendering virtuoso performances.

The whistle is usually associated with and is particularly suited to playing traditional dance music. Therefore, although detailed tuition on playing such music falls outside the scope of this book, a few tunes have been included to give the student a 'taste of what is on offer'. To begin, here is a tune that most folk enthusiasts are sure to recognise.

The double bar line preceded by two dots means that the section is to be repeated.

Chords used in this tune:

G   G7   C   A7   D7   D

28

Sweeney's Polka

Now try this Kerry polka from the south-west of Ireland.

Try using this alternative fingering to play G sharp. You will probably find it much easier to execute at high speed than half-holing.

Chords used in this tune:

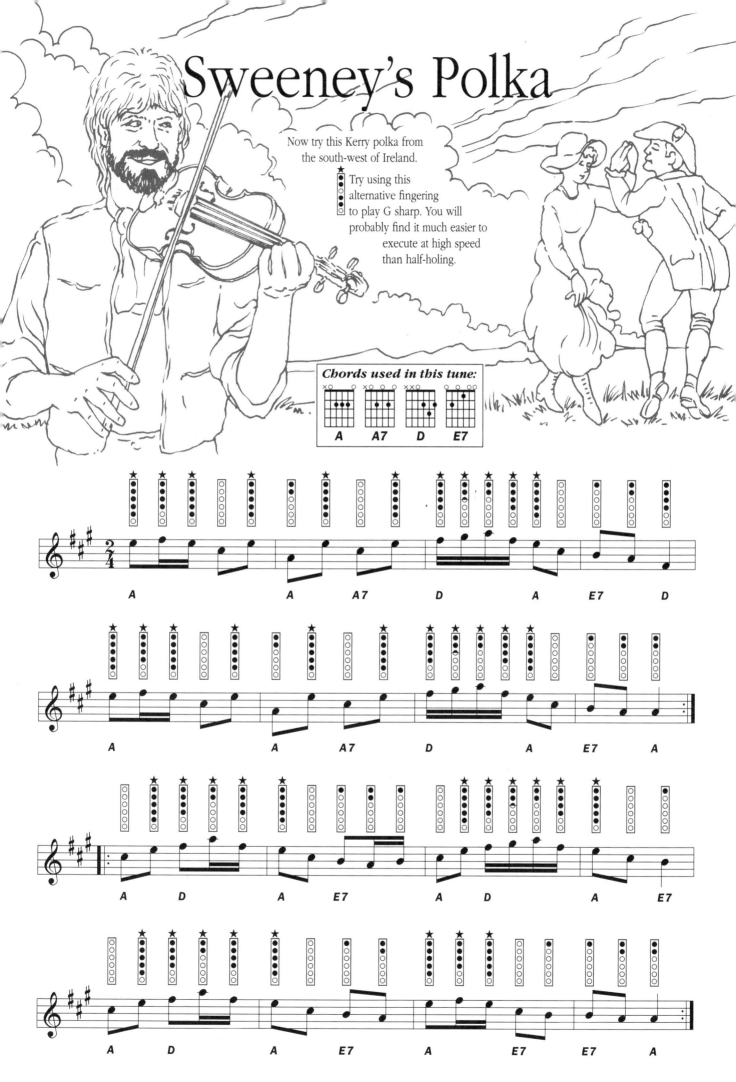

Oyster Girl

Traditional dance tunes in 6/8 time are called **jigs.** This jig is a great favourite with country dance bands. Cuts are of particular importance in this type of tune. Refer back to page 14 to jog your memory.

Captain Pugwash

Most people are familiar with the tune from the popular cartoon series 'Captain Pugwash'. The tune is a **hornpipe**, its proper title being **The Trumpet Hornpipe**. Hornpipes are characterised by a preponderance of dotted quaver/semiquaver pairs which sound like DAH DI.

The groups of notes enclosed by the curved line and a figure 3 above or below are called **triplets.** The three notes are played in the same time duration as two of the same value. These triplets are best played using the double-tongueing technique.

Soldiers' Joy

This tune is a reel. Of all the different types of dance tune, reels are definitely the most popular with musicians. You're sure to hear this reel played countless times at traditional music sessions in England. It is a tune which dates right back to at least the middle of the 17th century – some say it came from Scandinavia before that – and is sometimes called *King's Head*. 'Soldiers' joy' is reputed to be a euphemism for morphine.

Having reached this stage of the book means you must be serious about playing the tin whistle, so it is well worthwhile spending a little more money to progress further. There are still lots of things to learn that are well outside the scope of this book. You need to learn about *long rolls* and *short rolls*, *crans*, *double cut rolls*, *quadruplets* and a whole host of other specialist techniques. Among the many books that are available, three stand out in particular:

- **Tutor for the Feadóg Stáin** by Micheál Ó hAlmhain and Séamus Mac Mathúna, published by Comhaltas Ceoltóirí Éireann;
- **The Clarke Tin Whistle** by Bill Ochs, published by the Pennywhistler's Press (ISBN 0 9623456 0 1) and
- **Traditional Irish Tin Whistle Tutor** by Geraldine Cotter, published by Ossian Publications Ltd (ISBN 0 946005 12 5).

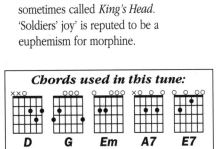

Chords used in this tune: D G Em A7 E7

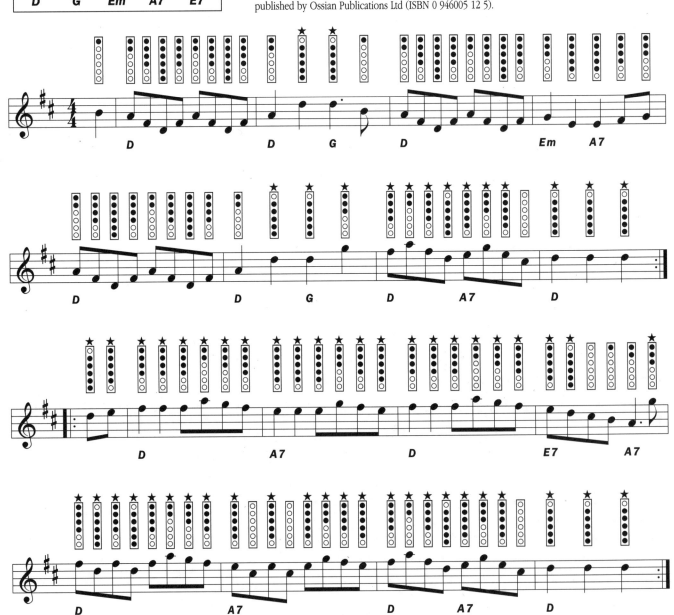